Icons of America

Steve Goldsworthy
and Heather Kissock

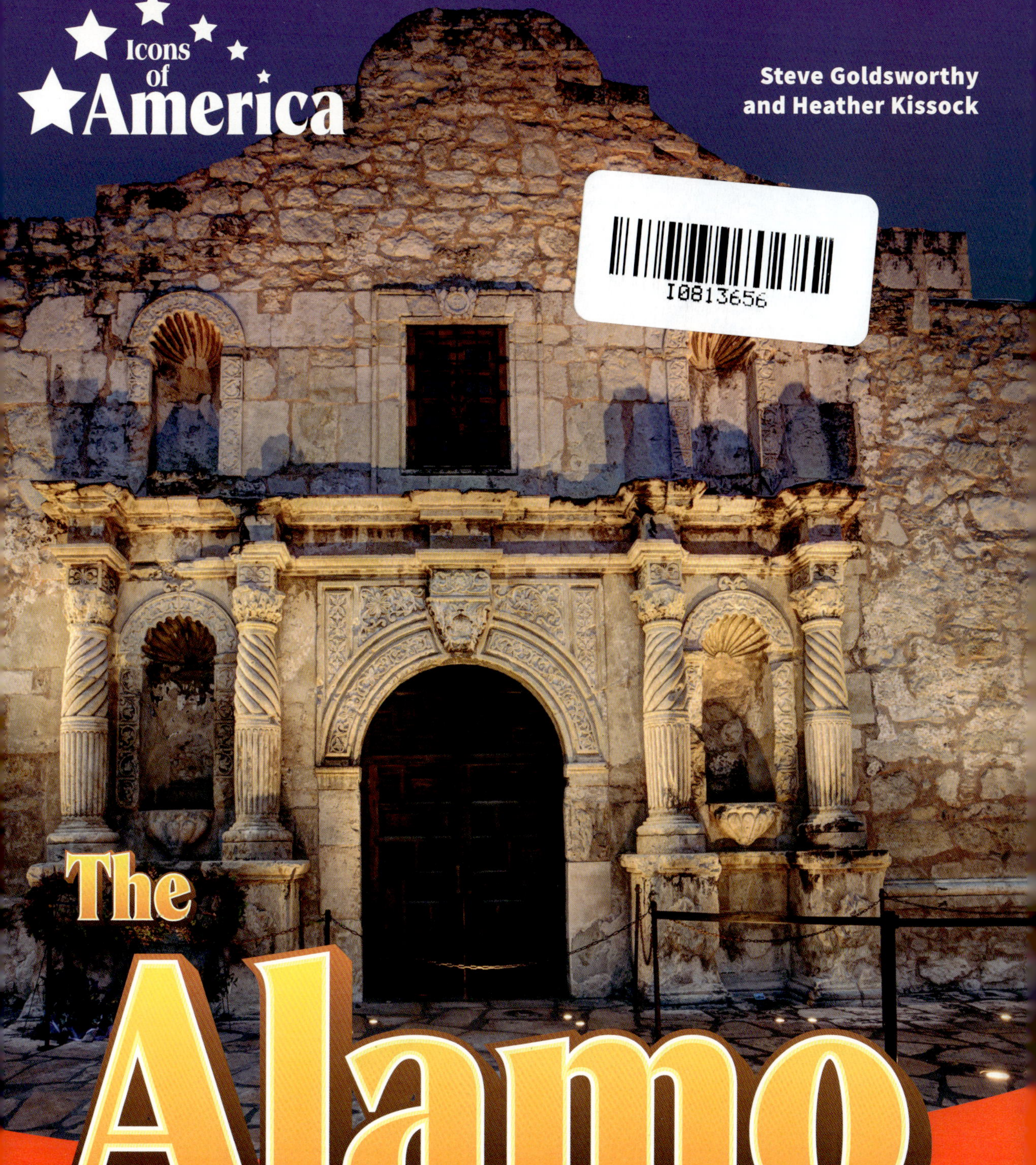

The Alamo

AV2
www.av2books.com

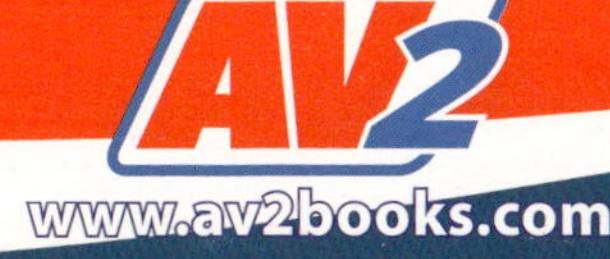

Step 1
Go to **www.av2books.com**

Step 2
Enter this unique code
ZUKXHYHNT

Step 3
Explore your interactive eBook!

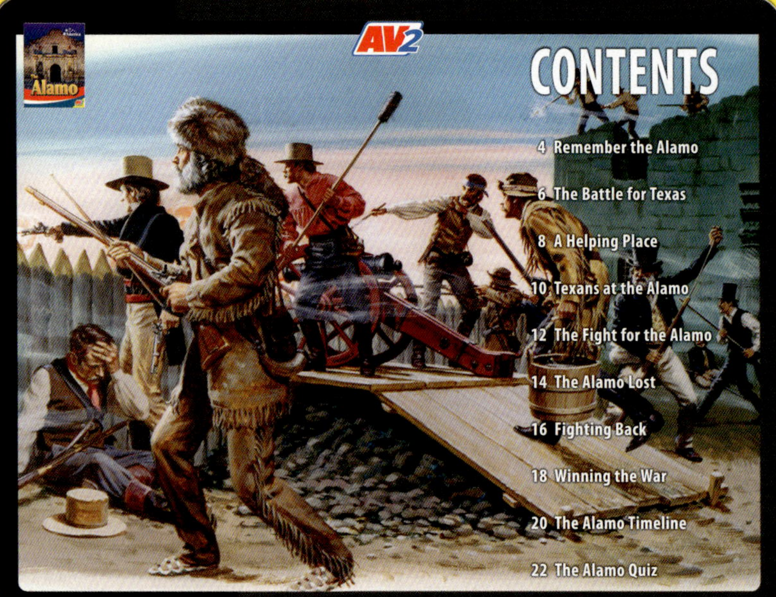

AV2 is optimized for use on any device

Your interactive eBook comes with...

Contents
Browse a live contents page to easily navigate through resources

Audio
Listen to sections of the book read aloud

Videos
Watch informative video clips

Weblinks
Gain additional information for research

Slideshows
View images and captions

Try This!
Complete activities and hands-on experiments

Key Words
Study vocabulary, and complete a matching word activity

Quizzes
Test your knowledge

Share
Share titles within your Learning Management System (LMS) or Library Circulation System

Citation
Create bibliographical references following the Chicago Manual of Style

This title is part of our AV2 digital subscription

1-Year 3–8 Subscription
ISBN 978-1-7911-3306-1

Access hundreds of AV2 titles with our digital subscription.
Sign up for a FREE trial at **www.av2books.com/trial**

The Alamo

CONTENTS

Remember the Alamo

The Alamo played an important role in Texas's fight for **independence**. It was the site of a major battle and tragic loss. However, this loss motivated the Texans to fight harder for their beliefs.

Over the years, the battle at the Alamo has come to represent the **heroism** and **resilience** of the Texan people.

Alamo means "**cottonwood tree**" in Spanish.

The Battle for Texas

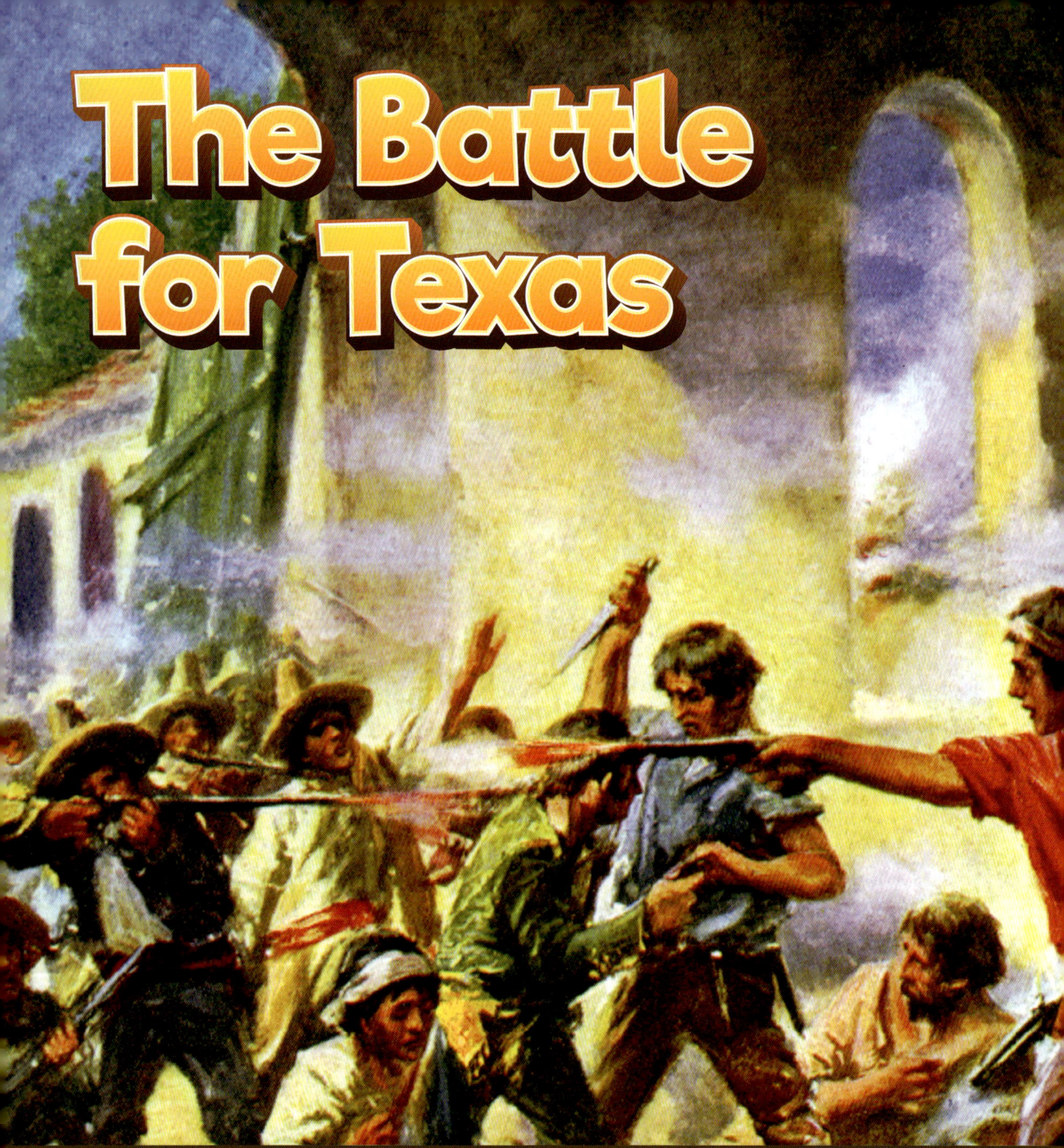

Texas has not always been part of the United States. In the early 1800s, the area was part of Mexico.

The Battle of Gonzales

Historians consider the Battle of Gonzales as the beginning of the Texas Revolution. The Texans won the battle after the Mexican soldiers retreated.

In 1835, new laws in Mexico led residents of Texas to seek independence. Mexico was not willing to cede the land, and the Texas Revolution began in October of that year.

A Helping Place

The Alamo was not built to serve a military purpose. It was built as a religious **mission** in the early 1700s.

The original complex was made up of several buildings, including a chapel, a residence for priests, barracks for the Native Americans working at the mission, and a textiles workshop. By the early 1800s, the mission was abandoned.

The Alamo became a **fort** in **1803**.

Texans at the Alamo

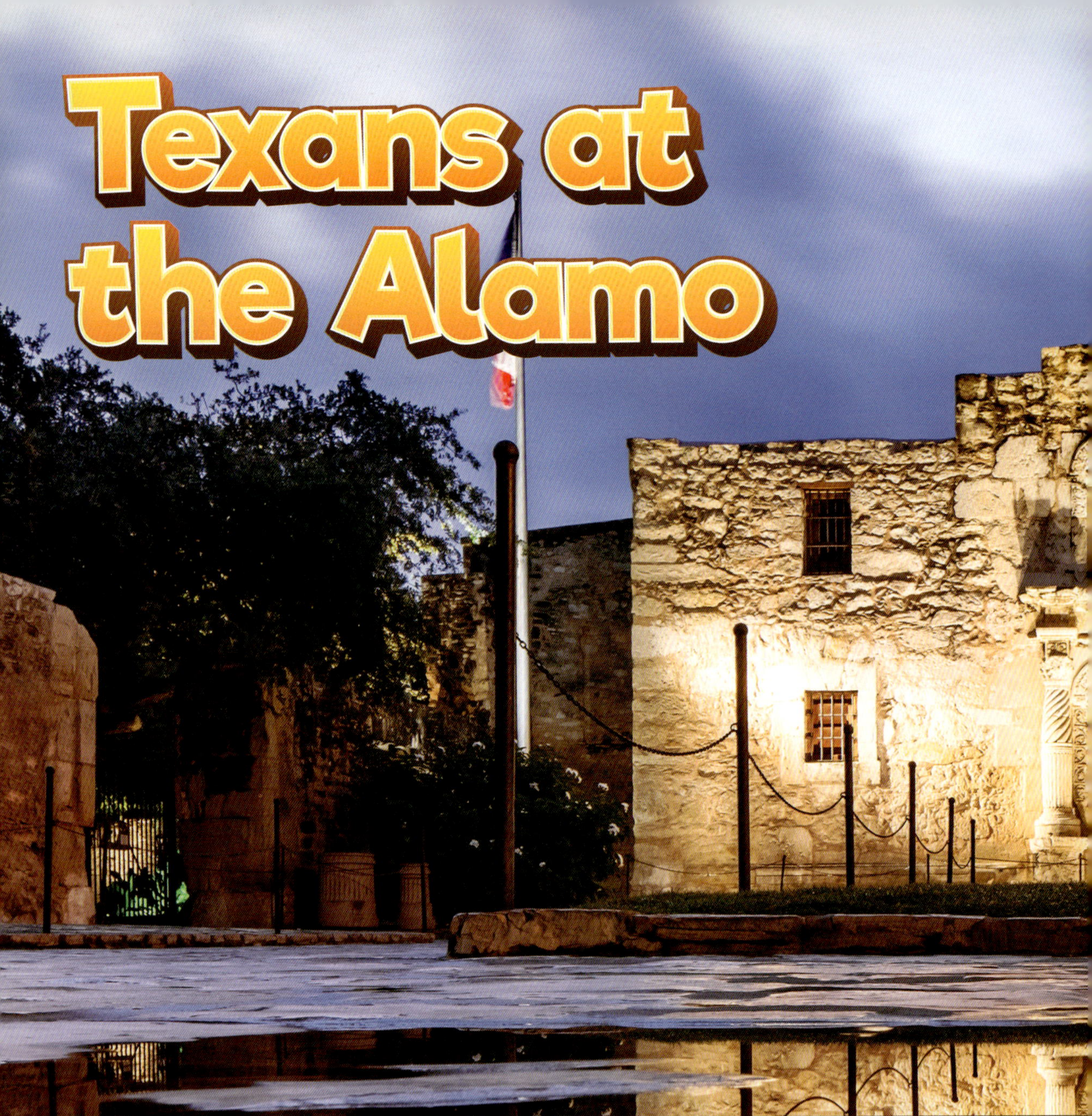

The Mexican army eventually took control of the Alamo, using it as a fort. The Alamo was situated at a crossroads and was a hub for commerce, so it held a **strategic** position for the people who controlled it.

Shortly after the revolution began, a battle took place in San Antonio. The Texans won the battle and took control of both the town and the fort.

The Fight for the Alamo

On February 23, 1836, Mexican troops arrived in San Antonio in an attempt to regain control of Texas.

The Mexicans were able to push the Texan fighters back across the San Antonio River. When the Texans reached the Alamo, they **garrisoned** themselves inside. The Mexican soldiers then launched their attack on the Alamo.

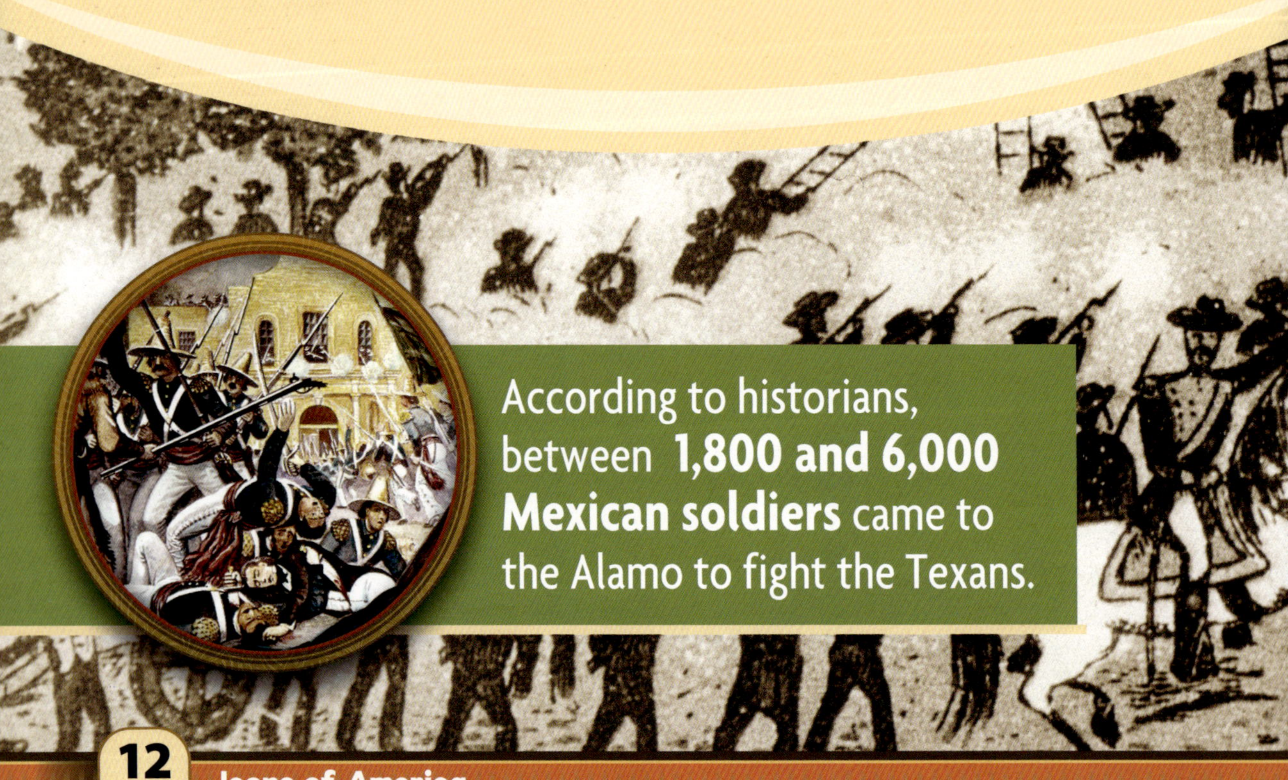

According to historians, between **1,800 and 6,000 Mexican soldiers** came to the Alamo to fight the Texans.

The Alamo Lost

Initially, the Texans were able to fend off the attack. However, on March 6, Mexican soldiers stormed the Alamo, climbing the walls and overwhelming the defenders.

More than 180 Texans died, and about 600 Mexican soldiers were killed or wounded. The dead included U.S. **frontiersman** and politician Davy Crockett.

Davy Crockett

Born in 1786.

Became a government worker in 1817.

Served for three terms in the U.S. Congress.

Fighting Back

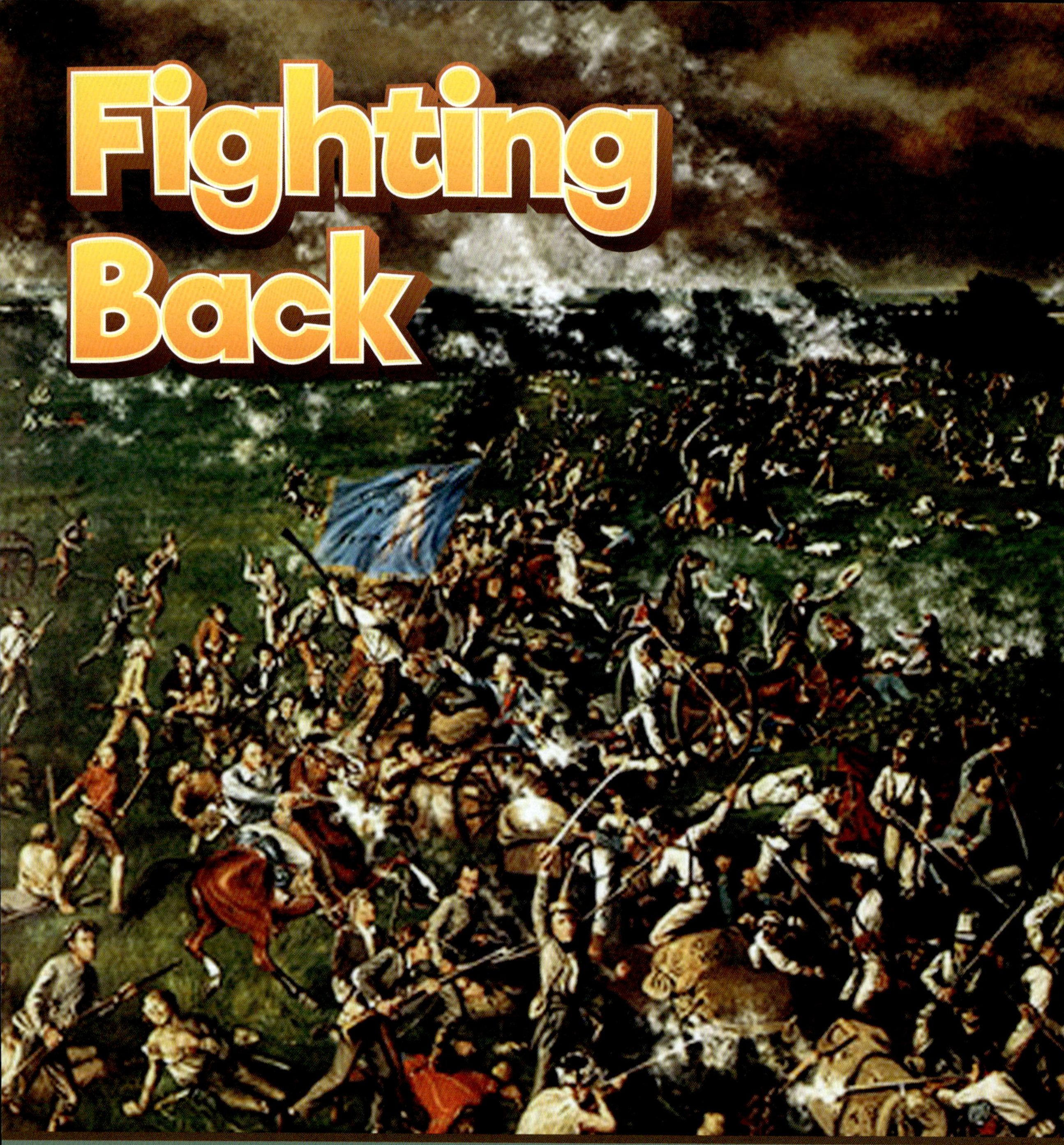

Instead of feeling defeated, the loss at the Alamo spurred the Texans to fight harder. It also inspired many Texans and Americans to join the fight.

During the final battle of the Texas Revolution, U.S. Army soldiers shouted, "Remember the Alamo!" This helped give them the push needed to fight the Mexican army.

Winning the War

The final battle of the Texas Revolution took place at San Jacinto in April 1836. The fighting lasted less than an hour, but in that time, the Texans were able to defeat the Mexican army.

Following Mexico's surrender, Texas became an independent republic. In 1845, Texas joined the United States as the 28th state.

The Battle of San Jacinto

The Battle of San Jacinto lasted for only 18 minutes.

About 900 Texan soldiers took part in the battle.

Only 9 Texan soldiers lost their lives.

More than 700 Mexican soldiers were captured.

The Alamo Timeline

1718	1803	1833	1835

Founding of the Alamo

Father Antonio de San Buenaventura y Olivares establishes the San Antonio de Valero Mission, later known as the Alamo.

Becoming a Fort

The San Antonio de Valero mission is turned into a fort.

President Santa Anna

Antonio López de Santa Anna becomes president of Mexico. He works to limit the freedom of Mexican states. U.S. residents of Texas are opposed to his plan.

The Battle of Gonzales

Hostilities between Mexicans and Texans break out with the Battle of Gonzales. The Texas Revolution begins.

1836

1960

2021

Texas Independence

Texans lost control of the Alamo in February. This defeat motivates them to fight harder. In April, they win the Battle of San Jacinto and obtain independence from Mexico.

The Alamo in Hollywood

Famed actor John Wayne directs and stars in a movie about the Battle of the Alamo. He portrays Davy Crockett.

A Cannon Replica

A full-size replica of a 7-foot- (2-meter) long cannon used during the Battle of the Alamo is unveiled on the Alamo site on April 16.

The Alamo Quiz

1 When did the Alamo become a fort?

2 Where did the last battle of the Texas Revolution take place?

3 When did Santa Anna become president of Mexico?

4 How many terms did Davy Crockett serve in the U.S. Congress?

5 What does the Spanish word *alamo* mean in English?

6 Who directed and starred in a 1960 movie about the Battle of the Alamo?

7 When did the Battle of Gonzales start?

8 When did Texas join the United States?

ANSWERS

1. 1803 **2.** San Jacinto **3.** In 1833 **4.** Three terms **5.** "Cottonwood tree" **6.** Famed actor John Wayne **7.** On October 2, 1835 **8.** In 1845

Key Words

frontiersman: a person who lives or travels in an undeveloped area

garrisoned: moved into a place in order to live there and defend it

heroism: great courage

historians: people who study the past by using different types of sources

hostilities: military actions in the context of a war

independence: freedom from the control and influence of other people or countries

mission: the place of residence of a group of people who teach religious beliefs and attempt to convince others of those beliefs

resilience: the ability to recover from difficulties or events that have negative consequences

strategic: carefully planned to achieve a particular goal

Index

Get the best of both worlds.

AV2 bridges the gap between print and digital.

The expandable resources toolbar enables quick access to content including **videos**, **audio**, **activities**, **weblinks**, **slideshows**, **quizzes**, and **key words**.

Animated videos make static images come alive.

Resource icons on each page help readers to further **explore key concepts**.

Published by AV2
276 5th Avenue, Suite 704 #917
New York, NY 10001
Website: www.av2books.com

Library of Congress Cataloging-in-Publication Data

Names: Goldsworthy, Steve, author. | Kissock, Heather, author.
Title: The Alamo / Steve Goldsworthy and Heather Kissock.
Other titles: Icons of America (New York, N.Y.)
Description: New York, NY : AV2, [2021] | Series: Icons of America | Includes index. | Audience: Grades 2-3
Identifiers: LCCN 2021007339 (print) | LCCN 2021007340 (ebook) | ISBN 9781791134945 (library binding) | ISBN 9781791134952 (paperback) | ISBN 9781791134969 (ebook)
Subjects: LCSH: Alamo (San Antonio, Tex.)--Juvenile literature. | Alamo (San Antonio, Tex.)--Siege, 1836--Juvenile literature. | Texas--History--To 1846--Juvenile literature. | San Antonio (Tex.)--Buildings, structures, etc.--Juvenile literature.
Classification: LCC F390 .G59 2021 (print) | LCC F390 (ebook) | DDC 976.4/03--dc23
LC record available at https://lccn.loc.gov/2021007339
LC ebook record available at https://lccn.loc.gov/2021007340

Printed in Guangzhou, China
1 2 3 4 5 6 7 8 9 0 25 24 23 22 21

042021
101120

Project Coordinator: Sara Cucini
Designer: Jean Faye Marie Rodriguez

Photo Credits
Every reasonable effort has been made to trace ownership and to obtain permission to reprint copyright material. The publisher would be pleased to have any errors or omissions brought to its attention so that they may be corrected in subsequent printings. AV2 acknowledges Getty Images and Alamy as its primary image suppliers for this title.